To my YesKid:
_____

With love from:
_____

MW00907195

Contents

Christian Media Publishers,
PO Box 4502, Durbanville, 7551
www.christianmediapublishing.com

Author: Ewald van Rensburg

Illustrations, Design & Layout: Lilani Brits

Publishing Project Manager: Noeline N Neumann

Reg No 2010/008573/07

Text: Maranatha Publishing: Used by kind agreement.

Printed in Malaysia through PrettyInPress Productions.

First Editon, second printing, 2013
ISBN 978-1-920460-52-5

CMP-kids books have been developed with your child's
(◉)) **developmental phases** and (✛) **unique temperament** in mind.
For a full explanation of the **unique temperament** and **developmental**
phases icons visit the CMP website **www.cmpublishing.co.za**

YesKids
Bible Stories
- about God's Greatness -

Kids saying YES! God is Great

Written by Ewald van Rensburg
Illustrations by Lilani Brits

cmp
christian media publishing KidS
pointing children in the **right direction**

1. My God is so great!
(Genesis 1 & 2)

God made our beautiful world.
First he made the light. He made the sun to shine in the day, and the moon and stars to shine at night. He also made the sea and the land. Then he made the plants and trees. There were flowers, fruit trees and vegetables everywhere.

Our great God also made
other things for this wonderful world,
like the fish that swim and
the birds that sing so sweetly.
He made the wild animals,
tame animals, insects and bugs.
Everything comes from God.

Then God did something very special ...
He made the first people. The man was
called Adam and the woman was called
Eve. The Lord loved them very much!

Come, let's pray together:

Lord, you are so great.
There is nothing that you can't
do. Thank you for making such
a beautiful world. Amen.

God made all the wonderful
things in the world.

2. Nothing is impossible with God!

(Genesis 12, 13, 15, 17, 18 & 21)

God told Abraham that he had to leave his home for another country. Abraham took his wife Sarah, and his nephew Lot with him.

They were happy for a while, but then Lot's workers and Abraham's workers began to argue. It's always so horrible when people fight.
So Abraham told Lot, "We must live in different places. You choose first where you want to live." Lot chose the best land for himself.

9

God had promised Abraham that he would care for him and give him a very big family; but Abraham and Sarah had no children.

They wanted children very much, but they were getting old. Had God forgotten his promise to them?

One day three men came to visit. They told Abraham that Sarah would soon have a baby boy. When Sarah heard this, she laughed. God wanted to know why she was laughing. Had she forgotten that God can do anything?

And a short while later a baby boy was born to Sarah and Abraham. They called him Isaac.

Come, let's pray together:

Thank you, Lord, that you care for me and that with you nothing is impossible. Amen.

God can do much more than people can! Nothing is impossible with him.

11

3. God is much stronger than Baal (1 Kings 18)

Elijah went to King Ahab and his fierce wife Jezebel. He said to them, "I am going to prove to you that God is much more powerful than your god Baal. Ask Baal to set this pile of wood on fire. I will ask God the same thing."

Nothing happened, Baal did not set the wood on fire. There was no sign of life from him at all. Then Elijah poured water onto his wood pile and prayed.

God set the sopping wet wood alight. Everyone saw that God was greater and more powerful than Baal.

Still Elijah was not finished. "God is going to make it rain now," he said. The sky was clear, except for a small cloud the size of a man's hand.

King Ahab and the rest of the people could not believe their eyes, as they watched the sky turned dark with rain clouds and it began to rain ... and rain ... and rain.

There is no one as powerful as our God.

Come, let's pray together:

Our Father God, thank you that you are so strong and so good to us. Amen.

God is great, and there is nothing that He can't do.

4. Five loaves and two fish

(John 6)

Many, many people wanted to hear Jesus talking about God. One day they listened to him until supper time, and the people were very hungry. They had forgotten to bring food with them.

Jesus told his friends to give the people food. Andrew, one of his friends, brought a small boy to Jesus. "This little boy has two fish and five loaves," he said. "But it's not nearly enough to feed this whole crowd of people."

Jesus smiled at the little boy and took the food from him. First, Jesus thanked his Father for the food. Then he shared it out among all the hungry people. And there was enough for everyone! It was a miracle. There was even food left over. Jesus' disciples collected twelve baskets of leftovers.

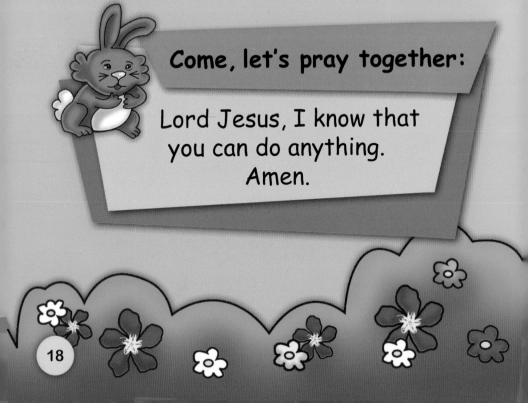

Come, let's pray together:

Lord Jesus, I know that
you can do anything.
Amen.

Jesus performed miracles that no person can ever do.

5. There is no one like Jesus

(Luke 8)

One day when Jesus was teaching a crowd of people about God, Jairus pushed his way to the front and fell to his knees. He said to Jesus, "My daughter is very ill. I know you can make her better." Jesus went with Jairus to his house. On the way there, people came running to meet them and told them that the little girl was already dead.

Jesus comforted Jairus. "Don't worry, just believe," he said.

When they reached Jairus' house Jesus told the people to stop crying. He told them the little girl was just asleep, but they laughed at him. Jesus went into the house. He took the little girl's hand and said, "Get up!"

Straight away she was better. Jesus told the family to give her something to eat. Everyone who saw her knew that there is no one like Jesus.

Come, let's pray together:

Lord Jesus, you really are wonderful. I love you very much. Amen.

There is no one like Jesus.
Remember, Jesus can
really help you.

Guidelines for parents

Faith Icon

The formation of faith is indeed unique to each child; there are however general characteristics which apply to all children. There are three main ways that children develop faith:

- Parents regularly reading the Bible, telling Bible and other faith based stories, praying together and doing faith building activities with their children (such as the ones found in this book).
- Children ask questions – parents need to take these questions seriously and answer them according to the child's level of understanding.
- Children follow the example of those caring for them.

Emotional intelligence icon

We experience emotions long before we learn the language to be able to express how we are feeling. Therefore it is important that children are taught to verbalise what they are feeling. Use the illustrations accompanying the stories and ask your child how they think the people or animals in the picture feel. This helps them become aware of their own emotions as well as those of others. It provides a learning opportunity where the child can learn appropriate words to express how they are feeling.

Reading icon

A wonderful world opens up for your child when they start learning to read. Enjoy every moment of this exciting adventure with your child. Let them sit on your lap where they can be comfortable and feel safe and secure. Open the book holding it so that you can both see the pages. Read clearly and with enthusiasm. As you know you can read the same story over and over. Point out where you are reading with your finger as you go along. This will help your child to begin to see the relationship between letters, sounds, words and their meaning. Encourage your child's attempts at reading – even of it sounds like gibberish.

Listening skills icon

Listening is an important learning and development skill. You can help develop this skill in your child by encouraging them to listen attentively, and understand what they are hearing. Let them look at the illustrations and then use their imagination to tell the story back to you in their own words. You can also encourage them to do this by asking questions relating to the story. Yet another way is to leave out words from a story the child knows well and let them fill in the missing words.

Vocabulary icon

Use every opportunity to build your child's vocabulary – it is a lifelong gift which you are giving to them. Start with everyday objects and people in the illustrations in books. Point at the picture, say the word, form a short sentence using the word. Repeat it again and then let your child say the word. Try to use the word in another context – if there is a tent in the picture you are looking at then say: we sleep in a tent when we go camping.

Numeracy skills icon

It is important for your child develop numeracy skills. Play simple games such as: "How many ducks are there in the picture? If we add two more ducks how many are there now? Then if three fly away? (use your fingers to illustrate this) How many are left? They also need to recognise the shape of numbers – cut large numbers from cardboard – let your child play with these – place the numbers in order forming a line from one to ten.